MW01542336

Nodus, Inc.
Debbie Waggoner
Decatur, TX

First published in 2020
Copyright © Debbie Waggoner 2020



The Connection Blueprint
Author: Debbie Waggoner
ISBN 978-1-7350283-0-9



www.nodus1.com

*For Robert, who always encouraged me to fly.*

*For our children, Andy, Laura and Kourtney,*
*who inspire me every day.*

*For my parents, who taught me everything.*

# TABLE OF CONTENTS

# INTRODUCTION

Over the past 25 years, I have provided leadership development to thousands of leaders. In leading a global talent development consulting business, I work directly with leaders at all levels who are striving to get better at developing high performing teams. Through training sessions, one-on-one coaching and talent development projects in start-ups to Fortune 100 companies and across a wide variety of industries, I've been privileged to support the success of many great leaders.

One day, I was working with a leader to identify good questions for her to use in one-on-one meetings to create strong engagement and openness. This leader was highly respected and had good rapport with her team, but she discovered that her employees weren't always open about concerns and requests. As I shared some important questions she could have been using in her one-on-ones, she said, "Can you just give me a list or a deck of questions? I don't have time to think of these each week!" From her request, the idea for this book was born.

The goal of writing this book is to provide an easy guide for leaders at all levels of the organization, from first-line supervisors to CEOs, to leverage effective one-on-one meetings with their employees. If you manage people, this book is for you.

I targeted one-on-one meetings because I have observed two key overlooked opportunities.

First, leaders often fail to leverage one of the best methods for leadership communication, the one-on-one meeting between a manager and an employee. For example, *The Ken Blanchard Companies & Training Magazine* surveyed over 700 training magazine subscribers in 2013. Key takeaways from this survey were that "89% of people want to meet with their manager on at least a monthly basis, with 44% of the people polled wanting to meet at least once per week. Only 73% of people actually do meet at least once a month. Only 34% of people actually meet at least once per week."[1]

You may be saying, "I talk to my employees every day; I don't need to have a scheduled one-on-one" or "I don't have time." Both may be true, but a one-on-one meeting is very different from daily interaction.

The one-on-one provides time for conversations that are more than just the problem of the day. It provides a focused time for you and your employee to get to know each other better, build a solid relationship, and discuss "how things are going" not just "what are you working on." And the time invested will pay off much more than many other activities such as responding to emails or attending another meeting.

In a recent *Harvard Business Review* article titled "How to Make Your One-on-Ones with Employees More Productive" by Rebecca Knight, there is a reference to Elizabeth Grace Saunders, the author of *How to Invest Your Time Like Money* and the founder of Real Life E Time Coaching & Training. She states:

> *"One-on-ones are one of the most important productivity tools you have as a manager. They are where you can ask strategic questions such as, are we focused on the right things? And from a rapport point of view, they are how you show employees that you value them and care about them."* [2]

They also ensure a scheduled time for the employee to bring up issues that they may be reluctant to discuss. Regularly scheduled one-on-one meetings have been shown to increase trust, transparency and engagement. If you want less turnover, more engagement and increased innovation, invest time in one-on-one meetings. They are a powerful tool for leaders.

A second observation is that even for those leaders who do have regular one-on-one meetings, many fail to ask great questions that lead to employee engagement and growth. Asking effective questions to coach and develop employees is a valuable leadership skill.

There are so many powerful questions that set the stage for a leader to motivate, engage and develop employees. But instead, many leaders give direction, instructions and background information, then expect the employee to remember everything and act on it. In other words, leaders do all the talking and should be doing more listening. This often occurs due to lack of skill and lack of time to plan or prepare. Is this you?

According to Julie Zhuo, author of *The Making of a Manager*, (Zuho, 2019, p. 66):

> *"The ideal 1:1 leaves your report feeling that it was useful for her. Remember your job is to be a multiplier for your people. If you can remove a barrier, provide a valuable new perspective, or increase their confidence, then you're enabling them to be more successful."*[3]

This book will enable you to seize these opportunities to connect and become a more effective leader. It includes a blueprint of sessions, questions and actions for an entire year. After you have read this book, you may be surprised to find that your preparation will only take an extra 5 minutes per week or an hour per month for each team member. Your time invested will also avoid many blow-ups, rework, conflicts and even turnover.

So, let's make it easy and practical for you to have great one-on-one meetings.

# HOW TO READ THIS BOOK

**Chapter 1**: Best practices – read this before starting.

**Chapter 2:** Start implementing these with a new employee. This provides specific questions for a new employee covering the first 90 days.

**Chapter 3:** Start implementing these with an experienced or tenured employee. These sessions can be used in any order and contain periodic checkpoints to review progress and make adjustments.

**Chapter 4:** This provides guidance for great one-on-ones for a virtual employee who is not in the same office or location as the leader.

**Chapter 5**: This addresses how to have one-on-one meetings with an employee who is not performing or is on disciplinary action.

**Chapter 6:** This addresses some common challenges that may occur in one-on-one meetings and provides ways to overcome these challenges.

**Chapter 7:** Get next steps to start using your one-on-ones to become a great leader.

**Index:** Search for a specific topic that you want to cover in a one-on-one meeting.

# 1

# Best Practices for One-on-One Meetings

Before you begin introducing or improving your one-on-one meetings, it's helpful to have these best practices in mind.

1) **Have a regular cadence and time –** For new employees (in their first 90 days), you may want to meet a couple of times a week or at the very least weekly. For more experienced employees, meet with them every two weeks, and for the most experienced employees and the more senior employees, once a month may work well. Thirty minutes to one hour is typically enough time for a regularly scheduled one-on-one meeting. One way to use your time effectively is to devote a third of the time for the employee, a third for job-related leader topics and a third for your discussion questions.

2) **Avoid cancelling –** Even though employees may say it's fine and may even say they don't need a one-on-one, they are needed, and cancelling says that something else is more important than your employee. Occasionally, that will happen. If so, work to get back on track as soon as possible. Cancelling regularly says that everything else is more important than this employee. Even if you think you don't have anything to discuss, use your scheduled time to just check in and get to know them more personally.

3) **Spend as much time listening as talking –** My husband is an introvert and dreaded his one-on-ones with his remote manager. He learned that his manager was building a pool and only had to ask him about his pool project. The manager then spent all his time talking about the pool

construction and soon their hour was up! (So, don't be the pool guy.) Do spend time getting to know each other personally and ask questions. Just don't do all the talking.

4) **Find a private place** – Your office, their office, a small huddle or conference room, or a coffee shop will work. If you want to get your daily steps in, invite them to take a walk around the building. Set aside your smartphone and laptop and really listen. Video is great for remote employees (you'll find more about this in Chapter 4).

5) **Take notes and follow-up** – Following up on action items or requests is a surefire way to build trust with each employee. Read aloud key takeaways and action items to ensure you are on the same page. Just be careful that you're not taking all the action items and doing all the documentation. Ask your employee to provide a short recap of key actions by sending an email to you after each session.

6) **Share ownership of the agenda** – Starting out, you will have the agenda of items to discuss. Ideally after about 90 days, ask your employee to bring their agenda and use your questions after they have covered their agenda. You are developing their skills in identifying priorities so the timing may vary. Both of you may email agenda items beforehand in order to allow time to prepare.

7) **Send questions ahead of time** – Especially if your employee is more introverted, they will value having time to think about the questions prior to discussing them. Send a short email the day before with the questions to consider for your next one-on-one. If there are any controversial topics, don't send them too far in advance as it may cause unexpected stress for the employee.

8) **Be careful about only discussing what's urgent today** – If you spend your time discussing current projects, customer issues or work problems, you will likely use all your time on these topics. Set allotted time for this, i.e. 20 minutes, and be willing to move on. This is time for a more general discussion of *how* things are going in order to coach and problem solve. The questions in this guide will prompt you to have a more meaningful, important, long-term discussion.

9) **Once a quarter, make it only about career development** – Often, our discussions about day-to-day topics, which we discussed in Best Practice #7, crowd out feedback and career development discussions. Reserve at least one meeting a quarter to provide more in-depth positive and constructive feedback and discuss the employee's career development.

10) **Adjust your style based on the employee** – As you apply these best practices and questions, you will need to observe each employee and adjust your approach based on their style. Some are more formal/informal, extroverted/introverted, detail-driven/big-picture-oriented, private/transparent, emotional/logical. Recognize that one size does not fit all so you can get the most out of your meeting with each person.

## Best Practices in Asking Questions

Asking questions effectively is a valuable leadership skill. Think of yourself as a coach/facilitator engaging and bringing out the best ideas from your employee. Use these best practices:

1) **Remember it's a discussion, not an interrogation** – If you don't get to all your questions, that's OK. The tone should be collaborative and one question may take longer to answer or open more opportunities for areas to discuss. Listening is just as important as asking.

2) **Watch your body language** – Open posture, good eye contact, no distractions (such as technology) and a pleasant demeanor all support positive communication. Your body language demonstrates whether or not you are truly listening and interested in what they have to say.

3) **Personal questions** – Everyone is different in the amount of personal information they are comfortable sharing and we should always respect an employee's privacy. Some employees share more than what you would like to know, while others prefer to not disclose personal information. If an employee shares too much, provide feedback and coaching on what is appropriate. (For example, hearing all

about their weekend escapades.) I recommend using some general questions to open the door and allow them to use it as they would like. For example, ask "How are things going outside of work?" rather than "How are you and your husband/wife doing?" As you build trust and learn more about your employee, certainly follow up on concerns or celebrations in their personal life. Just read them to make sure you are respecting them as an individual. And maintain confidentiality with each employee by not sharing what you learn with others.

4) **Avoid leading questions to get to the answer you want** – For example, you might say, "I think it would be a good idea if you tried X, what do you think?" You know the employee is going to say, "Yes, boss — great idea!" You are *not really engaging* them. Instead ask, "How would you approach this?" or "What ideas do you have for fixing this?" or "What might happen if you take that route?"

5) **"What else?"** – Often, the initial response after you ask a question is not everything and/or not deep enough. Asking "what else?" often gets to the heart of the matter or deeper insight.

6) **Evaluate the effectiveness of your questions** – Asking good questions is a skill that can greatly improve your ability to lead others. But be careful about asking a lot of "why" questions — you may come across as an interrogator. Avoid disguising advice or your ideas as a question. For example, "Have you thought about trying ______"? is not really a question. Remember the value of asking good open-ended questions that start with "what, where, when and how" and "tell me about."

## Best Practices in Structuring Your One-on-One Meetings

Let's get more specific about your meeting plan.

The format for each session includes a session goal, three discussion questions and a leverage point.

## EXAMPLE: SESSION 2

**Goal:** Build trust by getting to know the employee

**Discussion Questions:**

- ☐ What are you enjoying most about your job? Why do you enjoy it?
- ☐ Where are you having challenges/struggles?
- ☐ Who are you working with the most to get your job done? How is that going?

**Leverage Point:** Share one piece of positive feedback with the employee. Communicate the positive skill or behavior and the impact it is having on the team and the company.

A recommended overall agenda would be:

1) A couple of casual "How are you doing?" questions.

2) Ask the employee what they have on their mind, their agenda.

3) Your agenda including the discussion questions and leverage point.

4) Wrap up with action items.

The goal of the session is your intent or what you want to accomplish. Start out by asking the employee what they would like to discuss — any questions or issues they are having on the job. Then move to updates or information you need to share with them and your discussion questions.

The discussion questions should flow as a discussion in a collaborative way. Provide your comments and feedback as well. It should not be an interview, but a two-way conversation. Remember to listen. Use these questions as a guideline — sometimes you will not get to all questions but have other questions or topics to discuss.

These questions are great conversation starters and when you listen and fully engage with the employee, they will lead to a stronger relationship.

The leverage point is an additional perspective to add to your one-on-one if time allows and will create greater impact. It may be something for the leader to think about or discuss with the employee or an action for the leader to take.

Take notes and follow up with any action items by email.

"Checkpoints" are offered periodically for you to assess how your one-on-ones are going and how you may want to adjust or fine-tune them.

Now that you understand and can apply best practices when asking questions, you are ready to start using Chapters 2 and 3 to have great one-on-one meetings.

My goal is you keep this book at your desk or download it to your favorite e-reader. You might have a copy for each employee and take it to your meetings. Refer to it regularly to build a strong working relationship with every person who works for you.

I hope you're excited to get started!

# 2

# New Employee One-on-Ones

Let's start out with one-on-one sessions for new employees for the first 90 days on the job. These may also apply to someone new to your organization or new to a role. Your goal with new employees is to build trust by getting to know them, to provide structure and support so they can do their job well and to establish a culture of open communication.

Great one-on-one meetings are vitally important for new employees. These meetings are in addition to training sessions and giving day-to-day direction. Establishing a trusting relationship starts with your very first meeting. Use these questions to build trust and engagement. Set your phone aside, disengage from your computer and listen to let them know how much you value them.

After 90 days, move on to the sessions in Chapter 3.

**Goal:** Build trust by getting to know the employee

**Discussion Questions:**

- ☐ Tell me about your work background.

- ☐ Tell me about your life outside of work.

    *For personal topics, let the employee share as much or as little as they would like to. This is where you start building trust by listening and getting to know them as a person.*

    *Share your background as well to start building the relationship with this employee.*

- ☐ What do you need from me right now?

**Leverage Point:** Discuss or clarify your one-on-one meetings: overall goal, frequency, structure, role, content and confidentiality.

**Goal:** Build trust by getting to know the employee

**Discussion Questions:**

- ☐ What are you enjoying most about your job? Why do you enjoy it?

- ☐ Where are you having challenges/struggles?

- ☐ Who are you working with the most to get your job done? How is that going?

**Leverage Point:** Share one piece of positive feedback with the employee. Communicate the positive skill or behavior and the impact it is having on the team and the company.

## SESSION 3

**Goal:** Build trust by getting to know the employee

**Discussion Questions:**

- ☐ How are things going for you overall?
- ☐ What do you like to do for fun?
- ☐ How is your current work/life balance?

**Leverage Point:** Clarify what work is expected or not expected after hours. Discuss your personal view on work/life balance.

# SESSION 4

**Goal:** Leveraging strengths

**Discussion Questions:**

- ☐ What is something that comes really easy/naturally to you?
- ☐ How do you use that strength on the job?
- ☐ How can you use that strength more often or in other situations?

**Leverage Point:** Have your team take the StrengthsFinder assessment from Gallup to understand and discuss the use of strengths. (If you purchase the StrengthsFinder 2.0 book, the assessment code is inside). Discuss how you as a leader can use their strengths to support your weaknesses.

**30-DAY CHECKPOINT**

Ask each employee these questions after 30 days on the job.

- Have we done everything we said we would do?
- Have we done anything that made you think about leaving?
- Based on your experience at other jobs, what can we be doing better?

# SESSION 5

**Goal:** Role clarity and job satisfaction

**Discussion Questions:**

- ☐ Are you crystal clear on your role and what you should be working on? If not, what aspects aren't clear?

- ☐ What things about your current job do you enjoy the least? Why?

- ☐ What do you wish you would have known before you took this job?

**Leverage Point:** Observe the employee's body language. What is their posture, eye contact, gestures or voice telling you? Are they comfortable in your discussions? If not, what can you do to provide an open, relaxing environment? You could go for a walk or a coffee for a change of scenery.

**Goal:** Communication with employee and team communication

## Discussion Questions:

- ☐ What can help us improve daily communication in our team? What information do you need from me?

- ☐ Was there a recent team discussion or meeting where you didn't get to share your thoughts on a topic? You can share them here now....

- ☐ How are you most comfortable communicating? Email, face-to-face, phone, text?

**Leverage Point:** What would improve communication with this employee?

**Goal:** Team dynamics

## Discussion Questions:

- ☐ Who do you want to get to know better or work with more on our team? Is there anyone outside of the team you would like to network with?

- ☐ What's one conversation with a teammate that you've been avoiding having this week?

- ☐ How would you assess the level of communication and transparency on our team?

**Leverage Point:** Share feedback on the employee's ability to be an effective team member. Discuss your observations on successful team dynamics.

**Goal:** Stress management

**Discussion Questions:**

- ☐ What is one thing you have learned this week?

- ☐ What causes you the most stress?

- ☐ How is your stress level right now? How do you cope with or relieve stress?

**Leverage Point:** How can you gauge the stress level of this employee? What behaviors change when they are stressed and how do they change? (For example, some engage more with others when stressed, some withdraw.)

# SESSION 9

**Goal:** Build trust by getting to know the employee

**Discussion Questions:**

- ☐ Tell me more about your previous work experience and what you have been able to apply here.

- ☐ How are things going outside of work?

- ☐ What would you do if funds were unlimited? (What are your dreams?)

**Leverage Point:** Depending on how much the employee has shared with you about their personal life, take an interest in asking about their family, hobbies, etc. Respect their privacy if they are not open to sharing.

**Goal:** Career development

**Discussion Questions:**

- ☐ To help you do your job, what could you change about either your work environment or how you get your work done (soft skills*)?

- ☐ What soft skills* would you like to improve on?

- ☐ Who do you think models these skills at our company? What can you learn from them?

**Leverage Point:** Discuss how getting better at a soft skill has helped you as a leader.

*Soft skills might be communication, time management, influencing others, teamwork, accountability, leadership, etc.*

# SESSION 11

**Goal:** Recognition

**Discussion Questions:**

- ☐ What kind of recognition do you prefer?

- ☐ Is there any recognition you do not like?

- ☐ How would you describe our company to your family and friends?

**Leverage Point:** Discuss typical recognition on your team. (An example would be private vs. public praise). Clarify expectations of what exceptional performance looks like that would warrant recognition.

**Goal:** Connecting to the big picture/strategy

**Discussion Questions:**

- ☐ What's something good that happened to you this past week, at home or work?

- ☐ What do you do on a day-to-day basis that has the most impact on our company goals? *This is not a stump the chump question. Take the opportunity to explain the connection to make sure they understand how they make a difference.*

- ☐ What do we do today that does not add value to our customers/stakeholders?

**Leverage Point:** Provide an additional assignment for the employee to identify an internal or external customer that can provide additional perspective on the importance of this person's job or role within the company. Ask them to come back to you with what they have learned.

## NEW EMPLOYEE CHECKPOINT

Throughout your initial one-on-one sessions, you should be getting to know about the employee, their interests, motivations and personality. You should also be letting them know about you and your expectations. As you do so, the employee will open up more and you should find your one-on-ones more collaborative. Taking a personal interest in your employee should continue, so revisit this section and these questions periodically to build trust and engagement with each employee.

# 3

# Current Employee One-on-Ones

To implement one-on-ones with employees who have worked for you for some time, you may use some sessions from Chapter 2 to make sure you know them well and have established a trusting relationship. Sessions 13–50 do not have to be followed in order, but provide a nice variety of topics to engage the employee and establish a strong working relationship.

With experienced employees, you will want them to have more ownership in the one-on-ones by asking them to bring agenda items. Remember to use the overall agenda outlined in Chapter 1.

**Goal:** Goal setting

## Discussion Questions:

- ☐ What goals do you have for the next 90 days/6 months/year?

- ☐ What questions do you have about our team/department goals?

- ☐ How will setting goals and working to achieve goals support your career growth?

**Leverage Point:** Discuss how the employee might review goals on a regular basis and ways you can support their progress toward their goals.

# SESSION 14

**Goal:** Relationships with stakeholders

## Discussion Questions:

- ☐ Who are your most important stakeholders? Why are they the most important?

- ☐ How do they view you? How do you know (examples)?

- ☐ What stakeholder relationships would be most important to develop further?

**Leverage Point:** Prior to your one-on-one, gather informal feedback from stakeholders on your employee and share it with them or ask the employee to gather feedback from their stakeholders after the session.

# SESSION 15

**Goal:** Career development/resources

**Discussion Questions:**

- ☐ If you could choose a team member, leader or someone else at our company to coach you on a topic or who you would like to learn from, who would it be and why? *Work to make this happen.*

- ☐ Do you like to read? If so, what have you read lately? *Discuss books, blogs or websites that may support their job.*

- ☐ What or who inspired you this week?

**Leverage Point:** What ways can you expose employees to other leaders/subject matter experts? Buy a book for everyone on the team to read and discuss.

# RELATIONSHIP CHECKPOINT

Assess how your one-on-ones have been going with this employee by asking yourself these questions:

1) How would you define the relationship with this employee so far? How is the openness/trust/transparency?

2) How is the performance of this employee? Excellent, average, poor?

3) Continue to balance your time between building the relationship (getting to know them as a person, their work style and motivations) and their performance (clarifying expectations, providing feedback and coaching).

4) How much time are you talking in your one-on-one meetings? How much time is the employee contributing? It should be at least 50/50 working towards 30% you talking and 70% the employee talking.

**Goal:** Time management

**Discussion Questions:**

- ☐ What is your biggest struggle in managing your time?
- ☐ How am I impacting your ability to focus on your top priorities?
- ☐ What is a low priority item that takes a lot of your time?

**Leverage Point:** Brainstorm ways to eliminate time wasters. Share calendar/planning techniques.

**Goal:** Team relationships

## Discussion Questions:

- ☐ How are you impacting others on the team? How do you know?

- ☐ How could you contribute more to the team?

- ☐ How can you encourage others to contribute more?

**Leverage Point:** Consider what you have observed about this employee in team meetings and provide positive and constructive feedback on their contribution.

# SESSION 18

**Goal:** Improving efficiency

**Discussion Questions:**

- ☐ What might be some other ways to address challenging aspects of your job? What are we not thinking of?

- ☐ How could we be more efficient?

- ☐ Given all of your priorities, what can you say "no" to?

**Leverage Point:** Brainstorm ways to change processes or stop doing work of little or no value.

**Goal:** Career goals

**Discussion Questions:**

- ☐ What would your ideal job look like in the future?
- ☐ What would you like to work on more to get you to your future goal?
- ☐ Why is this important to you?

**Leverage Point:** Provide resources and time to support career development.

**Goal:** Quality standards

### Discussion Questions:

- ☐ How do you judge the quality of your work?

- ☐ How do you see your level of quality in comparison with others on the team in relation to what your customers expect?

- ☐ We can view our work as "A" quality, "B" quality and "C" quality. Tell me how you might determine when your work needs to be top "A" quality, medium "B" quality or just acceptable "C" quality.

**Leverage Point:** Make sure you clarify the quality standards expected and their top priorities based on quality of work expected. Discuss managing customer expectations around quality and response times.

**Goal:** Challenging problems or situations

**Discussion Questions:**

- ☐ Things did not go well this past week/month/day. What would you do differently?

- ☐ Who could you have asked for help to avoid these problems?

- ☐ What have you learned that you will apply in the future?

**Leverage Point:** View mistakes and problems as an opportunity for learning, not an opportunity for placing blame.

**Goal:** Coaching to take on a new task

**Discussion Questions:**

- ☐ How would you feel if you took on ___________?
- ☐ What would you need from me?
- ☐ How would you get started?

**Leverage Point:** Weigh the individual's experience and long-term goals when challenging them with more/different responsibilities. Some individuals may need to be encouraged to accept more responsibilities. When doing so, make sure you support them with frequent check-ins and coaching.

**Goal:** Creativity and innovation

**Discussion Questions:**

- ☐ Where can we be more creative in what we do?

- ☐ What helps you to be creative?

- ☐ Who do you consider to be very creative who you could spend more time with?

**Leverage Point:** Discuss ways to encourage creativity and innovation such as watching videos, brainstorming with others and experimenting.

**Goal:** Decision-making roles and responsibilities

**Discussion Questions:**

- ☐ What decisions do we need to make to move forward or are holding you up?

- ☐ How can we accelerate the decision-making process (discussion)?

- ☐ What decisions are you comfortable making on your own?

**Leverage Point:** Let the employee know what decisions you are comfortable with them making and what decisions should always come to you.

**Goal:** Communication methods and frequency

**Discussion Questions:**

- ☐ How is communication going overall for you? What modes of communication do we need to revise — email/text/calls?

- ☐ What do you need more/less information on?

- ☐ What do you think about our meeting/one-on-one timing and structure?

**Leverage Point:** Identify ways to change or improve how you both communicate.

## ONE-ON-ONE REFINEMENT CHECKPOINT

1) What is the employee bringing as agenda items? Do they need feedback or coaching on how to best use their time in one-on-ones?

2) How many one-on-ones have you cancelled? How can you ensure more consistency going forward?

3) How have you been doing at following up?

4) What have you learned about their motivations and working style?

**Goal:** Peer relationships

**Discussion Questions:**

- ☐ What is one thing you were able to do to support someone else in the past few weeks?

- ☐ What is the most meaningful part of your job?

- ☐ When do you have the most fun at work?

**Leverage Point:** Consider the culture of the team and how this employee positively or negatively impacts the culture. Provide feedback to the employee about their impact on the team.

**Goal:** Progress on goals

**Discussion Questions:**

- ☐ How are you progressing on your work goals and development goals?

- ☐ What are you most proud of?

- ☐ Where are you getting stuck on/not making progress with?

**Leverage Point:** Review their goals for the year or consider developing goals if they do not have any formalized. If they have goals in place and these goals have changed, make sure they are updated.

**Goal:** Stress management

**Discussion Questions:**

- ☐ How are you feeling about your workload today?

- ☐ What helps you stay on top of your priorities?

- ☐ How do you know when you are overloaded? Will you let me know?

**Leverage Point:** Be aware of verbal and nonverbal cues that let you know the workload and stress level of each employee. Examples might include complaining to others, being late, withdrawing from team engagement or demonstrating frustration.

**Goal:** Team relationships

**Discussion Questions:**

- ☐ Who do you find most helpful on the team?
- ☐ Who have you learned the most from?
- ☐ What can you teach/share with others to support their work?

**Leverage Point:** Encourage employees to reach out to peers more often for support and collaboration.

**Goal:** Provide feedback

**Discussion Questions:**

- ☐ What do you think you are getting better at? *Tie in to development goals.*

- ☐ *Share your feedback on #1.* How have you been able to make this improvement?

- ☐ What has been the impact of this improvement?

**Leverage Point:** Remember to take regular opportunities in the moment to give positive and constructive feedback on performance.

**Goal:** Feedback on your leadership

## Discussion Questions:

- ☐ What is something I can start doing as a leader to support you and your work?

- ☐ What is one thing I should stop doing that is getting in the way of our success?

- ☐ What should I continue doing to support you and the team?

**Leverage Point:** This is called "**Start, Stop, Continue**" feedback. Using this approach often provides more feedback to you from employees because it is structured. It may be helpful to send this to them to think about prior to your one-on-one meeting.

**Goal:** Company values

**Discussion Questions:**

- ☐ What company value is most important to you?

- ☐ What value do you think you need to work on?

- ☐ What are some ideas on how you could get better?

**Leverage Point:** Share your view on the company values and provide feedback on how this employee demonstrates or does not demonstrate the company values.

**Goal:** Meetings

**Discussion Questions:**

- ☐ What could we do to improve our meeting quality?

- ☐ What meetings could we eliminate?

- ☐ What are some creative ways we can make sure information is shared regularly without having a meeting?

**Leverage Point:** Review ongoing meetings and revise frequency, agenda and ownership of roles in the meeting so all employees develop meeting management skills.

## SESSION 34

**Goal:** Career development

**Discussion Questions:**

- ☐ What skill or areas of expertise do you have that we are currently overlooking?

- ☐ How could you use this skill to support the work of our team?

- ☐ What are some other ways or situations where you could use this skill or area of expertise?

**Leverage Point:** Be open to supporting the employee in implementing underutilized skills on your team or in the company. This may involve a shift in responsibilities or lead to project assignments.

# SESSION 35

**Goal:** Addressing challenges

**Discussion Questions:**

- ☐ What challenges are you facing and how can I help?

- ☐ What has worked in the past for you in addressing challenges like these?

- ☐ What have you tried already and what next steps are you considering?

**Leverage Point:** Don't provide your answer on how to address the challenge initially. Coach the employee to think of new options that may work better for them. Our inclination as leaders is to provide support by telling them what to do. Instead, coach them to come up with alternatives and to evaluate the pros and cons of each.

# SESSION 36

**Goal:** Time management/focus

**Discussion Questions:**

- What are the biggest distractions for you right now?
- What are some ways to manage these distractions?
- How can you either minimize them or get back on track quicker after a distraction or interruption?

**Leverage Point:** Discuss ways you have learned to manage distractions and interruptions.

**Goal:** Motivation

**Discussion Questions:**

- ☐ How can we maintain focus and excitement on our team?
- ☐ What inspires you to succeed every day?
- ☐ What is the biggest motivator for you?

**Leverage Point:** Discuss motivation at work and what you have learned about motivation.

**Goal:** Prioritizing

## Discussion Questions:

- ☐ Are there any big priorities you are not making progress on?

- ☐ What do you need to make progress?

- ☐ How can you adjust your time to move forward with this?

**Leverage Point:** Challenge the employee to show leadership skills by getting creative in managing their time to accomplish their priorities. Examples may include planning quiet time in a huddle room to work without interruptions, not attending every meeting or tackling bigger projects when they have more energy.

**Goal:** Competitor or industry insight

**Discussion Questions:**

- ☐ What are our competitors doing that we should be aware of?

- ☐ How can we become the company that would put us out of business?

- ☐ What would you change about our product/service if you could?

**Leverage Point:** Share how you use information, resources and articles from other industries to spark insight and innovation.

**Goal:** One-on-one meeting feedback

## Discussion Questions:

- ☐ What has been the most valuable aspect of our one-on-one meetings?

- ☐ What is one suggestion you have for change in our one-on-one meetings?

- ☐ On a scale of 1-10, how would you rate the quality and quantity of feedback I am providing for you in your job?

**Leverage Point:** Review cadence, structure and timing of one-on-one meetings.

## SESSION 41

**Goal:** Quality of work

**Discussion Questions:**

- ☐ How would you rate the quality of the work in our department?

- ☐ What could you do to improve the quality of your work?

- ☐ What could we do as a team to improve the quality of our work?

**Leverage Point:** Discuss the impact of quality on customers, stakeholders and company strategy. We are often not aware of how our work affects our reputation both internally and externally.

# SESSION 42

**Goal:** Connect work to the company strategy

**Discussion Questions:**

- [ ] What do you see as the connection between your work and our department goals? Business unit goals? Company goals?

- [ ] What would you like to know more about relating to our company?

- [ ] Do you consider yourself more strategic or tactical? Why?

**Leverage Point:** Discuss company strategy and the role the department plays in achieving this strategy.

# SESSION 43

**Goal:** Feedback

**Discussion Questions:**

- [ ] What is the most important feedback I have given you this year?

- [ ] What makes it easy or hard for you to receive feedback?

- [ ] Do you feel comfortable asking for clarification if you don't understand the feedback I provide?

**Leverage Point:** Consider what you know about the employee and how they receive both positive and constructive feedback, and share your insights in this discussion. Being open to feedback is critical for career success. There may be opportunities for you to adjust your approach as a leader or for them to work on being more open.

# SESSION 44

**Goal:** Build trust by continuing to take an interest in the employee

**Discussion Questions:**

- ☐ What are you doing these days that is fun for you outside of work?

- ☐ What has been your all-time favorite vacation? Why?

- ☐ What helps you de-stress?

**Leverage Point:** Discuss current or new personal interests to stay engaged and interested in the employee. We don't get to know everything in the first 90 days and our lives and interests change over time.

**Goal:** Tools and technology

**Discussion Questions:**

- ☐ What tool or technology is the most valuable for you in your job right now?

- ☐ How can you learn more about this technology or tool?

- ☐ What can you teach others about it?

**Leverage Point:** Discuss the balance of technical skills and soft skills in their overall job performance. Share which you see as more important and why.

## SESSION 46

**Goal:** Prioritizing

**Discussion Questions:**

- ☐ Which of your priorities are competing right now?

- ☐ What does that look like?

- ☐ Who could you be talking to (besides me) in order to align priorities?

**Leverage Point:** Provide guidance where needed in aligning priorities and also encourage the employee to partner with other stakeholders to align priorities.

**Goal:** Change management

**Discussion Questions:**

- ☐ What change has been the most challenging for you?
- ☐ What was especially hard about it?
- ☐ How have you been working through this?

**Leverage Point:** Discuss the emotional aspects of change. We have a logical response to change and an emotional response. We may need to let go of the old way in order to embrace the change even if we see it as a good idea. Talking through a change can help process the emotional side.

**Goal:** Conflict strategies

**Discussion Questions:**

- ☐ Where has the most conflict occurred in getting your job done?

- ☐ How have you dealt with this conflict?

- ☐ How could you deal with it better in the future?

**Leverage Point:** Discuss ways to bring up difficult subjects with peers and work through conflict. Recommended resources are *Crucial Conversations* by Al Switzler, Joseph Grenny, and Ron McMillan or *Radical Candor* by Kim Scott.

**Goal:** Assess challenge level

**Discussion Questions:**

- ☐ Are you being challenged enough in your job? Too much?
- ☐ What challenges do you enjoy the most?
- ☐ Where do you need more support?

**Leverage Point:** As a leader, you should allow time for employees to struggle some in order to learn and innovate. If you jump in too soon, they may become dependent on your knowledge and experience. It's important for them to know when to ask for help as well.

## SESSION 50

**Goal:** Project review

### Discussion Questions:

- ☐ What metaphor or analogy would you use to describe this past year/project?

- ☐ What are you most proud of?

- ☐ When have you had the most fun?

**Leverage Point:** This may come as a separate conversation, as part of an annual performance conversation or at the end of a project. A debrief provides an opportunity to apply lessons learned to the next year or new challenge.

# EMPLOYEE ENGAGEMENT CHECKPOINT

1) How would you define the relationship so far? How is the openness/trust/transparency?

2) How is the performance of this employee? Excellent, average, or poor?

3) What are their strengths and areas of opportunity?

4) What is the biggest opportunity for growth for this employee?

5) How does their current role align with their career goals?

# 4

# Virtual Employee One-on-Ones

One-on-one meetings with virtual employees are even **more important** than with face-to-face employees. Without regular communication, it's easy for virtual employees to get off track with priorities, roles and responsibilities and communicating regularly to others. Establish a cadence of regular one-on-ones to engage virtual employees and allow them to be the valuable resource they can be.

Ideally, one-on-one meetings are face to face. Leaders should take every opportunity when they travel to the employee's location to plan time for a one-on-one individual meeting. These are critical as there is nothing that can truly replace face-to-face communication for building trusting relationships.

The second-best option for virtual one-on-one meetings is to use video. Since the COVID-19 pandemic, many teams have used video for meetings, yet some are still reluctant to use it for one-on-ones. Even with the quality of video technology improving significantly, there is a tremendous amount of reluctance to use this great communication tool. In many organizations, we have to literally "rip the tape off" the webcam to start the process of using video.

Over time, you will find that the ability to communicate is much more effective using video, but you will need to persevere before it's seen as a benefit. I've never heard of a leader who introduced using video to their team and got a response like "Great, we are so excited to try video for our one-on-one meetings!" Instead you'll often hear groans and "Do we have to?" You will also need to give it several tries to get comfortable with the technology from both sides. Over time, you and your team will see the value of observing body language and having a more focused session.

Be reasonable about time zones. Don't expect employees to take an after-hours or very early call by video. And don't introduce video for the first time in a high conflict conversation where you need to provide constructive feedback, or at a performance review. Use it for some casual conversations consistently before using it for more challenging communication.

Your third option is the phone. On a phone call, in addition to your agenda topics, your role is to listen for what's not being said. Pay special attention to tone of voice and inflection. Follow up with the employee any time you think something may be misunderstood or off-track. In order to listen at this level, you need to remove all distractions and really focus on the employee.

Building relationships virtually is first done by following through consistently and doing what you say you will do. Your virtual employees learn that you value them through your follow-up to their emails, requests and information needed. Over time, you can build a personal relationship, but it will take longer. To start and maintain positive virtual relationships, be vigilant about following up to gain their trust.

# 5

# Using One-On-Ones to Resolve Performance Issues

When you have learned or observed a performance issue with an employee, start by providing a clear description of the discrepancy between expectations and performance. The guidelines in this chapter are for when you first learn of a performance issue or if you are having your first or second meeting on the topic. Often, performance issues are really about unclear expectations so it's important to always start with clarifying the expectations of their job. This section is not attempting to provide guidance on more serious disciplinary discussions.

You want to accomplish two things in this one-on-one meeting:

1) Be clear about what you have seen/observed/ become aware of so they are aware of what they need to do differently.

2) Let them know you care about them as a person and will support them in addressing this situation.

Don't avoid these conversations. The longer you wait, the more difficult they are and the harder it is for the employee to make the changes needed. Do your homework and learn as much as you can about the situation to be prepared for this meeting. Focus on facts and if possible, observe the performance yourself.

Earlier, we recommended sending questions in advance of the one-on-one meeting. When you identify a performance issue, I recommend you let the employee know the topic you would like to discuss but not necessarily specific questions. If you suspect they may be worried or concerned about this meeting (which is very likely), don't send the topic too early to create more time for them to stress about it. Send a meeting invite with the topic either the afternoon before or 3-4 hours in advance of the one-on-one. This may be done as part of your regular one-on-one meetings or may be a separate meeting depending upon the urgency of the situation.

Plan to identify the topic you would like to discuss and briefly describe what you have observed. Then engage the employee — what is their view? What information can they provide? They almost always have some information or insights that you were not aware of. Work together to come up with a plan to address the issue and use the employee's suggestions as to how to address it.

Watch your tone of voice and body language. You may be frustrated or upset, and communicating this does not help the conversation. Your goal is to maintain respect and provide clear, direct feedback that provides an opportunity for the employee to improve. Use a straightforward tone of voice and take the time to really listen to their view.

Questions to address performance issues:

1) Let's discuss the expectations of your role. What do you see as your most important priorities right now?

2) What's getting in the way of you accomplishing X?

3) Our agreement was for you to do X and that is not being done. Can you give me some insight into why you have not been able to accomplish this?

4) Do you understand why this is important? Clarify the impact of this work.

5) What can you do differently? What can you do to accomplish this?

6) How will this change/help/modify your results?

7) What is your plan going forward? Let's review the next steps.

8) How can we best measure this?

9) What support do you need from me?

10) What challenges do you foresee?

11) How might you overcome these challenges?

12) What other resources could be helpful?

Establish a specific follow-up date and/or check-in time. This will vary based on the issue. Don't micromanage the situation but also don't ignore it and not follow up. Provide guidance and support through regular check-ins and discussion about progress or challenges. An example would be, "I'll check in with you on Tuesday and Thursday afternoon at 3:00 p.m. to see how it's going and what questions or concerns you have."

Ask the employee to summarize your conversation by email and send it to you. This will allow you the opportunity to ensure clear understanding and an agreed upon action plan.

End with communicating your confidence in their ability to resolve the issue and your commitment to support them in doing so.

# Troubleshooting One-on-Ones

Even the best leader can experience challenges in one-on-one meetings. Here are the most common challenges with solid recommendations and a place for note taking.

| Common Challenge | Recommendations | Notes |
| --- | --- | --- |
| Employee is very quiet, does not engage in conversation in the one-on-one | Send questions ahead of time. | |
| | Communicate to them that you would like their input. | |
| | Provide positive feedback when they contribute. | |
| | Allow time to build trust, slow down your pace. | |
| Employee talks too much | Provide feedback on their need to be more concise. | |
| | Allow time to build trust with this employee. | |
| | Agree on a visual clue such as a hand up or gentle interruption to help them learn when they need to stop or pause. | |
| | Discuss the importance of recognizing when they are talking too much in other situations at work. | |

| Common Challenge | Recommendations | Notes |
|---|---|---|
| Employee spends most of the time complaining | Ask them to come to the next meeting with a solution to their complaint. | |
| | Let them know you expect them to come with solutions, not just problems. | |
| | Point out that your time together is valuable and discussing things that can't be resolved is not using that time most effectively. | |
| | Stop them politely when they are complaining. | |
| Your schedule is crazy and you have to keep cancelling your one-on-one meetings | Plan your one-on-ones further ahead, six months to a year on your calendar. | |
| | Get creative, do them over lunch, breakfast, in the car or between external meetings. | |
| | Recognize that how you spend your time is the #1 way employees know what is important to you. | |
| | Cancel other meetings or delegate them. | |
| The employee tells you they are experienced and don't need a one-on-one | Acknowledge their experience but don't take it as an excuse. | |
| | Find a cadence that works — bi-weekly or monthly may work for someone very experienced. | |
| | Using the questions in this book will engage even someone very experienced who doesn't like one-on-one meetings! | |

| Common Challenge | Recommendations | Notes |
| --- | --- | --- |
| You don't have time to prepare | With this book, you can prepare in 5 minutes. Identify your objective for the meeting, choose questions to ask from Chapters 2 and 3 and ask the employee to update you on one thing that's going well, one challenge and one update. | |
| You don't feel that your meetings are effective – you don't see results | One-on-ones are a slow down to speed up process. These are one of the best ways to build trust and this happens over time. Providing a way for an employee to bring up concerns or issues has a significant impact on their engagement, so be patient. It will pay off! | |
| | Use the one-on-one checkpoint questions on page 48 to ask the employee how they are doing and develop ways to improve their effectiveness. | |
| | Review the Best Practices of One-on-Ones and Best Practices of Asking Questions in Chapter 1 to identify areas to adjust. | |
| Lack of documentation or no time to document | Ask the employee to send a short follow-up email after each one-on-one with bullet points of what you discussed and any action items, owner and due date. | |

| Common Challenge | Recommendations | Notes |
| --- | --- | --- |
| The one-on-one meetings are uncomfortable to end | Thank them for their time. Review any agreed-on action items and share documentation by email. Let them know you enjoyed it and leave the door open for them to contact you. | |
| The employee has more experience than you | They may have more technical experience but you likely have more leadership experience and experience working cross-functionally. | |
| | Always acknowledge their technical experience and provide positive feedback for their contribution. | |
| | Provide feedback on their soft skills as much or more than their technical skills. | |
| | Work together to support their career goals. | |

| Common Challenge | Recommendations | Notes |
|---|---|---|
| Employee spends the majority of their time pointing fingers or complaining about other employees | Be transparent and reflect back what you are hearing from them. For example, if someone is complaining too much, you might say, "In our last four meetings, you have spent most of our time complaining about X. Do you think that this is best use of our time together?" | |
| | Ask them to think about what they are doing that is impacting the situation and what they can change and come back to you with their suggestions. | |
| | Let them know you want to spend your time discussing their role and their job to help them develop. | |
| | Roleplay conversations they could have with others to address the situation. | |

Don't let challenges discourage you. It's much easier to address challenges in a one-on-one with an employee than have them surprise you or impact job performance. Keep in mind your goal to build a trusting relationship and match your approach to the employee.

# 7

# Next Steps

As a leader, you have many things that demand your time and attention, yet the most important thing you can do is invest in the relationship with your employees. We all continue to be challenged to do more with less. Only through leveraging your team and collaborating on what is most important will you be able to navigate these challenging, exciting times as a leader.

Here are some recommendations for applying what you've learned in *The Connection Blueprint*:

- Let your employees know you are going to start having regular one-on-one meetings, the purpose of them and their role in the meetings and discuss the frequency and time frame. Get them in your calendar. Be open to adjusting the time and frequency if needed.

- As you move along with your sessions, check the sessions you have already had and note the date you had that discussion. Put a star by questions that you really like and add your own questions that you develop as well.

- Once a week, review your priorities for the week, which should include your upcoming one-on-one meetings and the status of each of your employees. Are they engaged? Are they performing the job well? Are they ready for more challenges?

- Use the checkpoints in Chapters 2 and 3 to reflect, engage the employee and adjust.

- After one year, the questions will still apply so start over. You may decide to change the order or find ways to have the employee engage more as well.

I am excited to provide a true blueprint for connection in your leadership and for leaders globally. I would love to hear how you are using this guide for your one-on-ones and the impact it's having on your team and organization.

Contact me at **www.nodus1.com**

I challenge you to be known in your organization and with people who work for you as the leader who has the best one-on-ones and truly invests time and interest in their employees. You are leaving a legacy, so let it be one of career growth, incredible performance and most of all significant relationships.


Debbie Waggoner

Nodus, Inc.

**www.nodus1.com**

# INDEX

# Questions Organized by Session Goal

# REFERENCES

[1]Diehl, J., Houson, D., Witt, D., Zigarmi, D. (2013, October 13). Employee Passion, Vol 6. *Are Employees' Needs Being Met by One-on-Ones? Survey Says "NO".*
Retrieved from https://www.kenblanchard.com/getattachment/ Leading-Research/Research/Employee-Passion-Volume-6/ Blanchard-Employee-Passion-Vol-6.pdf


[2]Knight, R. (2016, August 8). *How to Make Your One-on-Ones with Employees More Productive.*
Retrieved from https://hbr.org/2016/08/how-to-make-your-one-on-ones-with-employees-more-productive


[3]Zuho, J. (2019). *The making of a manager: what to do when everyone looks to you.* New York: Portfolio/Penguin.